Idaho

BY ANN HEINRICHS

Content Adviser: Stephanie Bailey-White, Public Information Officer, Idaho State Library, Boise, Idaho

Reading Adviser: Dr. Linda D. Labbo, Department of Reading Education, College of Education, The University of Georgia

COMPASS POINT BOOKS MINNEAPOLIS, MINNESOTA

Compass Point Books
3109 West 50th Street, #115
Minneapolis, MN 55410

Visit Compass Point Books on the Internet at *www.compasspointbooks.com*
or e-mail your request to *custserv@compasspointbooks.com*

On the cover: Challis National Forest

Photographs ©: Photo Network/Bill Terry, cover, 1; Link/Visuals Unlimited, 3, 40; Unicorn Stock
Photos/Jean Higgins, 5; Gary C. Will/Visuals Unlimited, 6, 11; Buddy Mays/Travel Stock, 8; John Elk III,
9, 22, 29, 35, 36, 39, 42, 43 (top), 47; Photo Network/Mark Newman, 10; Mark E. Gibson/Visuals
Unlimited, 12; Robert McCaw, 13, 44 (top), 48 (top); Unicorn Stock Photos/Mark E. Gibson, 14;
Hulton/Archive by Getty Images, 15, 18 (bottom), 19, 20, 34, 46; North Wind Picture Archives, 16, 17,
18 (top), 41; Courtesy of Idaho Power Company, Boise, Idaho, 21; Photo Network/Patti McConville, 25;
Mark E. Gibson/Image Finders, 26, 45; Corbis, 27, 28; Sharon Gerig/Tom Stack and Associates, 30;
Unicorn Stock Photos/Chuck Schmeiser, 31; Corbis/Kevin R. Morris, 32; Corbis/James L. Amos, 33;
Kevin & Betty Collins/Visuals Unlimited, 38; Robesus, Inc., 43 (state flag); One Mile Up, Inc., 43 (state
seal); John Sohlden/Visuals Unlimited, 44 (middle); PhotoDisc, 44 (bottom).

Editors: E. Russell Primm, Emily J. Dolbear, and Patricia Stockland
Photo Researcher: Marcie C. Spence
Photo Selector: Linda S. Koutris
Designer: The Design Lab
Cartographer: XNR Productions, Inc.

Library of Congress Cataloging-in-Publication Data
Heinrichs, Ann.
  Idaho / by Ann Heinrichs.
      p. cm. — (This land is your land)
Includes bibliographical references (p.) and index.
ISBN 0-7565-0352-3 (alk. paper)
  1. Idaho—Juvenile literature. [1. Idaho.] I. Title.
  F746.3.H45 2003
  979.6—dc21   2002155726

Table of Contents

NOTE: In this book, words that are defined in the glossary are in **bold** the first time they appear in the text.

Welcome to Idaho!

Meriwether Lewis and William Clark crossed Idaho in 1805 and 1806. The state's lofty mountains gave the explorers quite a challenge.

"We were entirely surrounded by those mountains," Clark wrote. Without knowing the area, it seemed "impossible ever to have escaped." They crept along "steep sides of tremendous mountains entirely covered with snow."

Much of Idaho is still as the explorers found it. Some of America's most rugged wilderness areas are in Idaho. The Rocky Mountains cover much of the state.

Many hardy **pioneers** made their way into Idaho. Some came looking for gold, silver, and other minerals. Some cut logs from the dense forests. Others came to farm. They made Idaho America's top producer of potatoes.

Today, farming, logging, and mining are still important **industries.** Idaho's factories also make computer parts and many other goods. Tourism is also an important industry.

Thousands of visitors come to Idaho every year. As modern-day explorers, they enjoy this vast wilderness. Now come explore Idaho, too!

▲ Petit Lake is located in Sawtooth National Recreational Area in the Rocky Mountains.

▲ The Snake River makes up part of Idaho's western border.

Idaho is one of the mountain states. It's located in the northwest part of the United States. It's sometimes considered part of the Pacific Northwest.

Northern Idaho borders Canada. To the west are the states of Washington and Oregon. Nevada and Utah lie to the south. On the east are Montana and Wyoming. The narrow, northern part of Idaho is called the Panhandle.

Most of Idaho's border with Montana is a crooked line. This line follows mountaintops along the Continental Divide. Rivers west of this line flow into the Pacific Ocean. Those to the east reach the Mississippi River.

Idaho's western border is straight except for the middle section. Here, the

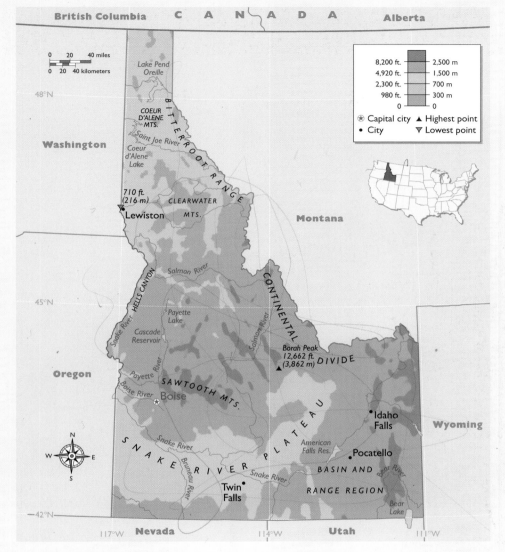

Legend:
- 8,200 ft. / 2,500 m
- 4,920 ft. / 1,500 m
- 2,300 ft. / 700 m
- 980 ft. / 300 m
- 0 / 0
- ⊛ Capital city
- • City
- ▲ Highest point
- ▽ Lowest point

British Columbia · C A N A D A · Alberta

Washington

Lake Pend Oreille

COEUR D'ALENE MTS.

BITTERROOT RANGE

Saint Joe River

Coeur d'Alene Lake

710 ft. (216 m)
Lewiston

CLEARWATER MTS.

Montana

Salmon River

HELLS CANYON

Snake River

Payette Lake

Cascade Reservoir

CONTINENTAL DIVIDE

Salmon River

Borah Peak 12,662 ft. (3,862 m) ▲

Oregon

Payette River

Boise River

Boise ⊛

SAWTOOTH MTS.

Idaho Falls

Wyoming

SNAKE RIVER PLATEAU

Snake River

Bruneau River

American Falls Res.

Snake River

Pocatello

BASIN AND RANGE REGION

Bear River

Twin Falls

Bear Lake

Nevada · Utah

117°W · 114°W · 111°W

48°N · 45°N · 42°N

▲ **A topographic map of Idaho**

Snake River forms a natural boundary. The Snake River is a tributary, or branch, of the Columbia River. The Columbia flows into the Pacific Ocean.

▲ **Hells Canyon forms part of Idaho's border with Oregon.**

Hells Canyon on the Snake River is the deepest **gorge** in the United States. It's even deeper than Arizona's Grand Canyon. Boise is Idaho's state capital and its largest city. It lies along the Boise River, which flows into the Snake River.

Much of Idaho is a rugged, mountainous wilderness. The Rocky Mountains cover almost half the state. They extend from Canada to south-central Idaho. Many mountain ranges within the Rockies run through the state. They include the Bitterroot, Clearwater, Coeur d'Alene, and Sawtooth Mountains.

▲ **The Sawtooth Mountains**

▲ Bruneau Dunes State Park is located near Mountain Home in southwestern Idaho.

The southeastern corner of the state lies in the Basin and Range region. It is dry and desertlike, with low mountains and gravel-covered valleys.

Southern and western Idaho are on the Snake River **Plateau.** The Snake River sweeps in a big curve through this high, level plain. Sagebrush and other tough plants grow on the plains. Much of Idaho's best farmland lies in the Snake River valley. Most of Idaho's people live in the valley, too.

The Snake River Valley is full of strange land formations. **Mesas** and **lava** beds spread across the landscape. Craters of the Moon National Monument is in south-central Idaho. This area is so rough that it reminds people of the Moon's surface. It has more than thirty craters of

▲ **The Snake River**

▲ **Visitors hike through the Craters of the Moon National Monument.**

volcanoes that are no longer active. Many hot-water

springs lie underground in Idaho. In fact, some buildings

in Boise get their heat from these hot springs.

Forests of pine and fir cover Idaho's mountains. These

trees give the state a booming wood industry. Elk, moose,

and mule deer roam through the woods. Grizzly bears, timber wolves, and cougars lurk in the forests, too. Mountain goats and bighorn sheep scamper across the rocky mountainsides.

▲ **Mountain goats live on Idaho's rocky mountainsides.**

▲ Skiers enjoy Mount Baldy in Sun Valley.

Many cold-water fish thrive in Idaho's rivers and streams. Grays Lake National Wildlife Refuge is in southeastern Idaho. Scientists there are trying to reintroduce endangered whooping cranes.

The high mountains get the coldest weather and the most snow in Idaho. People from all over the world come to Idaho's Sun Valley to ski. The eastern mountains also protect the state in the winter. They hold back frigid air that sweeps through Montana.

The Snake River Plateau is quite dry. Farmers grow crops there using irrigation. Southwest Idaho gets the warmest summer weather. In the mountains, though, even summers are cool.

Idaho was a Native American hunting ground for thousands of years. In the north were the Kutenai, Salish, Coeur d'Alene, and Nez Perce. Paiute people lived in west-central Idaho. The Shoshone and Bannock occupied the south.

Family groups lived in villages. They moved as the seasons and food supplies changed. They caught salmon, hunted wild game, and gathered forest plants. Many tribes worked together to hunt buffalo. They dried the meat to eat

▲ Shoshone Indians lived and hunted in southern Idaho.

during the winter. Buffalo skins were made into warm blankets and robes.

The first white people in Idaho were American explorers.

▲ **White settlers nursing an ill Native American in the 1840s**

Meriwether Lewis and William Clark arrived in 1805. They were on a westbound **expedition** to reach the Pacific Ocean. Fur traders and **missionaries** soon followed. Traders opened a trading post on Pend Oreille Lake in 1809.

Gold seekers rushed through present-day Idaho during the California Gold Rush of 1849. The year before, Idaho had become part of America's Oregon Territory. In 1853, it was split between Oregon and Washington Territories. Idaho was soon to have its own gold rush. Gold was discovered on Orofino Creek in 1860. Two years later, more gold turned up near Boise. Idaho Territory was finally created in 1863.

Thousands of new settlers poured into the territory. They followed the Oregon Trail and crossed deserts, mountains, and dangerous rivers. Many settlers were Mormons—members of the Church of Jesus Christ of Latter-day Saints.

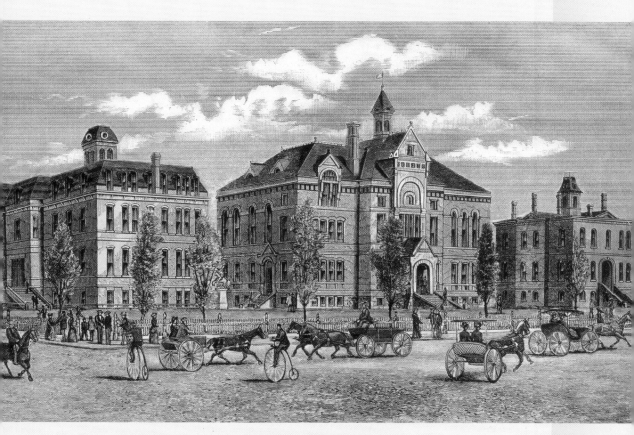

▲ **Boise in 1862, at about the same time gold was discovered there**

▲ Chief Joseph led the Nez Perce.

They often clashed with other Christian groups. In 1860, Mormons founded Franklin, Idaho's first permanent settlement.

Idaho farmers irrigated their land and began growing potatoes. In the mountains, miners dug out lead and silver. Meanwhile, the U.S. Army was moving Idaho's Native Americans to **reservations.** Many Native Americans fought for

▲ The U.S. Army during a struggle with Native Americans near Owyhee River in the late 1800s

▲ Loggers in Ola in 1939

years to keep their homelands. Chief Joseph of the Nez Perce gave up his brave struggle in 1877.

Idaho became the forty-third U.S. state in 1890. Many miners joined labor unions to get better working conditions. Violent fights often broke out between miners and mine owners. In the early 1900s, logging became an important industry.

During World War II (1939–1945), Idaho produced food and metals as war supplies. Japan was one of America's enemies in the war. The U.S. government feared that Japanese

Americans were a danger to America's security. Thousands of men, women, and children were rounded up and imprisoned in camps. In Idaho, almost ten thousand Japanese Americans were held at Camp Minidoka.

After the war, Idaho's manufacturing industries grew. The U.S. government also opened the National Reactor Testing Station near Idaho Falls. There, in 1951, electricity was first generated from nuclear energy. Brownlee, Oxbow, and Hells

▲ Japanese Americans were kept in camps such as this one in Rupert during World War II.

▲ **Brownlee Dam was built on the Snake River.**

Canyon Dams were built on the Snake River. They brought water-powered electricity to the region.

Two terrible disasters struck in the 1970s. A fire broke out in the Sunshine Silver Mine in 1972. More than ninety people died in the fire. In 1976, Teton Dam near Rexburg burst. Its floodwaters killed eleven people.

Today, tourism is a growing business in Idaho. State leaders are working hard to keep Idaho's air and water clean. They also struggle to solve disputes among various groups. Loggers and developers want to expand their activities. At the same time, **environmentalists** want to protect Idaho's natural areas.

When Idaho became a territory in 1863, its capital was Lewiston. Then Boise became the capital in 1865. At one point, the citizens of Hailey protested. They wanted Hailey to be Idaho's capital. Boise won, however. Today, the dome on the state capitol rises high over downtown Boise.

▲ **The state capitol in Boise**

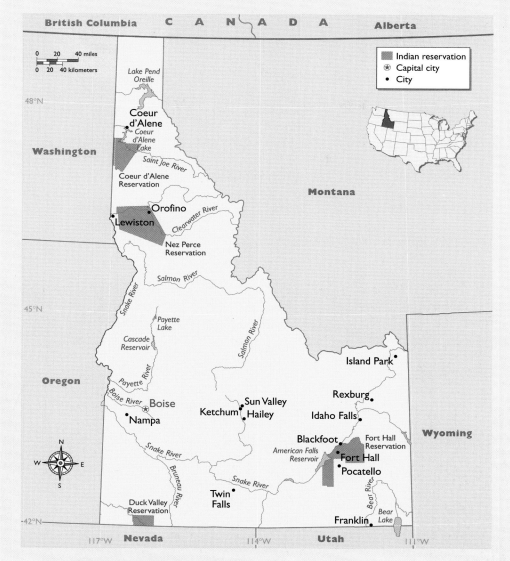

A geopolitical map of Idaho

Idaho's state government is divided into three branches—
legislative, executive, and judicial. The U.S. government is
organized the same way. Having three branches makes for

a good balance of power. Each branch makes sure that no other branch gets too powerful.

The legislative branch makes the state laws. Idaho voters elect lawmakers from the district where they live. The lawmakers serve in Idaho's state legislature. It consists of a thirty-five-member senate and a seventy-member house of representatives. The lawmakers meet in the state capitol in Boise.

The executive branch makes sure the state's laws are carried out. Idaho's governor is the head of the executive branch. Idahoans vote to choose a governor every four years. Voters also elect six other important executive officers. The governor appoints the heads of several departments. These include the department of agriculture and the board of education.

The judicial branch is made up of judges and their courts. The judges hear cases in court. Then they consider whether someone has broken the law. Idaho's highest court is the state supreme court. Voters elect its five justices, or judges. The judges decide which one will be the chief justice.

Idaho is divided into forty-four counties. Voters elect three commissioners to govern each county. They also elect a sheriff and other county officials. Most Idaho cities elect a mayor and a city council.

▲ **A fountain in front of city hall in Boise**

▲ Potatoes are an important crop for Idaho.

You've probably eaten potato chips or mashed potatoes recently. If so, you were likely eating an Idaho product. Idaho grows more potatoes than any other state.

Idaho is famous for one special potato—the Russet Burbank potato. The plant scientist Luther Burbank developed it in the 1870s. (*Russet* means reddish-brown.) The Russet Burbank is oval shaped, with shallow "eyes," or buds. Its skin has tiny lines that look like a net.

After potatoes, hay and wheat are the most valuable

crops. Idaho ranks second in the nation in production of barley, sugar beets, and lentils. It's also one of the top sources for milk.

Beef cattle are the leading farm animal. They graze on ranches that stretch across the plains. Many farmers raise dairy cattle and sheep. You might be surprised to hear about another Idaho farm animal—trout! Idaho raises more trout than any other state.

Manufacturing is Idaho's major industry. Computer equipment and other electronics are the top factory goods.

▲ Beef cattle are Idaho's leading farm animal.

Boise's Micron Technology manufactures microchips, which help computers run.

Foods, wood products, and chemicals are important products, too. Food plants process Idaho's many farm products. They make potato chips, refine sugar beets, and package meat and milk. Idaho's forest trees yield tons of lumber. Boise is the home of one of America's leading producers of wood products.

Idaho's nickname is the Gem State. Its most famous gem is the beautiful star garnet, the state gemstone. Other gems found in Idaho are jade, opals, jasper, agates, and topaz. Idaho's mines also yield phosphate

▲ **One of Idaho's many farm fields**

rock, sand, and gravel. Silver is another valuable mineral. Gold is still mined in the state, as well.

Tourism is an important industry in Idaho. It's one of the state's many service industries. Tourists visit Idaho for its ski resorts and beautiful scenery. It takes a lot of people to care for tourists' needs. Other service workers may include store clerks, teachers, truck drivers, lawyers, and health care workers.

▲ **Tourists admire Shoshone Falls.**

Suppose Idahoans were spread out evenly across the state. There would be about sixteen people per square mile (six per square kilometer). However, much of the state has no residents at all. Many rugged areas don't even have roads. People can reach them only by foot or on horseback.

The 2000 census counted 1,293,953 people in Idaho. That made it thirty-ninth in population among all the states. Almost

▲ **Few people live in this part of the Sawtooth Mountains near Stanley.**

half of all Idahoans live outside of cities and towns.

Most residents live in southern Idaho's Snake River Valley. That's where the largest cities are. Boise is the capital and largest city. Next in size are Nampa, Pocatello, and Idaho Falls. Coeur d'Alene and Lewiston are major cities in the Panhandle.

Mormons are Idaho's largest religious group. Southeastern Idaho has several Mormon communities. They have strong ties with Utah, where the church's headquarters are located.

More than nine out of ten Idahoans are white.

▲ A waterfall in front of a Mormon temple in Idaho Falls

Other residents are **Hispanic,** Native American, Asian, and African-American. Idaho's major Native American groups are the Nez Perce, Shoshone, Kootenai, and Coeur d'Alene. The largest Native American reservation is Fort Hall Reservation, near Pocatello.

Many Idaho towns hold rodeos. Nampa's Snake River Stampede is one of the largest rodeos in the West. The Lewiston Roundup is another big rodeo. Lumberjack Days in Orofino celebrates loggers' skills. People compete in sawing, chopping, and rolling logs. Boise holds the Western Idaho State Fair. The Eastern Idaho State Fair is in Blackfoot.

▲ A cowboy rides a bull at the Teton Valley Rodeo in Tetonia.

The Shoshone-Bannock Indian Festival takes place at the Fort Hall Reservation. Expert dancers from different tribes gather there. They perform to the sound of drums and songs. The festival includes a rodeo, pony races, storytelling, and games. The Nez Perce Reservation also hosts powwows and other cultural events.

Idaho's Basque people hold folk festivals in Boise. They celebrate their culture with music, dancing, food, and games. They came from the Basque region of northern Spain. Many Basques settled in Boise after arriving in the

▲ Native Americans in traditional dress dance at the Shoshone-Bannock Indian Festival.

▲ **Author Ernest Hemingway lived in Ketchum.**

United States. In fact, Boise and its surrounding area are home to the largest population of Basques outside of Europe. You can learn more about Basque history and culture at the Boise Basque Museum and Cultural Center.

Many authors came from Idaho or have lived there. Carol Ryrie Brink was a children's book author. She was born in Idaho and became an orphan at an early age. Her most famous book was *Caddie Woodlawn* (1935). It tells the story of her grandmother as a pioneer girl.

Vardis Fisher wrote about frontier days in Idaho. His novel *Mountain Man* (1965) was made into the movie *Jeremiah Johnson.* Ernest Hemingway was a famous author of novels and short stories. His story *The Old Man and the Sea* (1952) won a Pulitzer Prize. Hemingway moved to Ketchum in 1960. He died and was buried there in 1961.

Would you like a real explorer's experience? Then hike the Lolo Trail. Lewis and Clark followed this trail in Idaho. They were cold, hungry, and wet as they crossed the rugged Bitterroot Mountains. If you want to be more comfortable, you can retrace their route by car.

Nez Perce National Historical Park spreads across four states. Idaho's park center is in Spalding. (For the Nez Perce, the town's name is Lapwai.) There you'll find movies and museum exhibits about Nez Perce history and culture. Tour the site, and you'll see burial grounds, battlefields, and food-gathering fields. In some places, you'll hear tales of Coyote. This legendary spirit turned other creatures into stone.

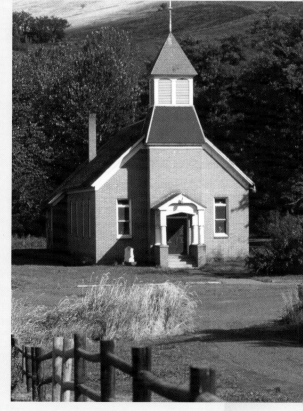

▲ **Spalding Church is part of the Nez Perce National Historic Site.**

In Boise, you can tour the huge state capitol. If the lawmakers are meeting, you're welcome to watch them in action. The Idaho State Historical Museum is in Boise, too. Wander among its exhibits on Native American and pioneer life. Then tour the museum's Pioneer Village. The Discovery Center of Idaho is another great place to visit. You'll explore the mysteries of science in its many hands-on exhibits.

Near Murphy is the Silver City Historical Area. It was once a silver-mining "boom town." Silver City is often

▲ **A visitor at the Discovery Center of Idaho in Boise**

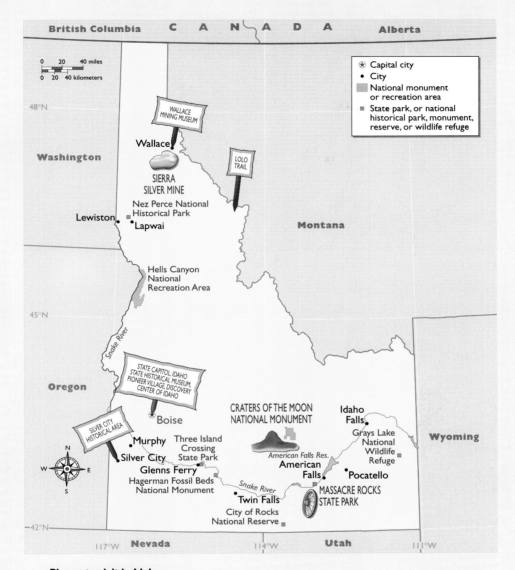

Map labels:

British Columbia — C A N A D A — Alberta

0 20 40 miles
0 20 40 kilometers

48°N

Washington

Capital city
• City
National monument or recreation area
■ State park, or national historical park, monument, reserve, or wildlife refuge

WALLACE MINING MUSEUM

Wallace

LOLO TRAIL

SIERRA SILVER MINE

Montana

Nez Perce National Historical Park

Lewiston • Lapwai

Hells Canyon National Recreation Area

45°N

Snake River

Oregon

STATE CAPITOL, IDAHO STATE HISTORICAL MUSEUM, PIONEER VILLAGE, DISCOVERY CENTER OF IDAHO

SILVER CITY HISTORICAL AREA

Boise

CRATERS OF THE MOON NATIONAL MONUMENT

Idaho Falls

Murphy   Three Island Crossing State Park

Silver City

Glenns Ferry

Hagerman Fossil Beds National Monument

American Falls Res.

American Falls

Grays Lake National Wildlife Refuge

Wyoming

Pocatello

MASSACRE ROCKS STATE PARK

Snake River

Twin Falls

City of Rocks National Reserve

42°N

117°W   Nevada   114°W   Utah   111°W

▲ **Places to visit in Idaho**

described as the "queen of Idaho's ghost towns." Wallace was another old mining town. Today, you can tour its Sierra Silver Mine and Wallace Mining Museum.

▲ **City of Rocks**

From an airplane, Craters of the Moon looks like a black wasteland. There's plenty to explore on the ground, though. Cone-shaped hills called cinder cones rise above the surface. There are bumpy lava fields and chunky rock piles. Each formation was created from violent explosions deep within the earth.

City of Rocks looks just like its name. It's a cluster of towering rocks, stone arches, and caves. Pioneers passed through the "city" on their westward trek. You can still see where they wrote their names on the rocks.

One famous route through Idaho was the Oregon Trail. You can see ruts left by the wheels of covered wagons.

They're visible at two state parks—Massacre Rocks in American Falls and Three Island Crossing in Glenns Ferry.

Did you know there were horses 3.5 million years ago? Their skeletons were discovered at Hagerman **Fossil** Beds. The Hagerman horse is the earliest parent of today's horses, donkeys, and zebras. It's also Idaho's state fossil. Today, you can tour Hagerman Fossil Beds. You'll see where horses, saber-toothed cats, and other prehistoric creatures were found.

▲ **A skeleton of the Hagerman horse, Idaho's state fossil**

▲ **Visitors enjoy a hike through Idaho's scenic mountains.**

For a wild ride, take a raft or boat through Hells Canyon. The Snake River churns and swirls for miles through this gorge. Maybe you prefer a calmer experience. If so, hike through the vast wilderness area surrounding the canyon.

You'll ramble among high peaks, desertlike river bottoms, and grassy meadows. You'll see bighorn sheep and mountain goats scrambling across the rocky hillsides. Look up, and you're likely to catch a glimpse of falcons circling high overhead. As you take in the nature all around you, you're sure to agree that Idaho is a great state to explore.

Important Dates

1805	Meriwether Lewis and William Clark are the first white people to enter Idaho.
1809	David Thompson builds a trading post on the bank of Lake Pend Oreille.
1834	Fort Boise and Fort Hall open.
1860	Gold is discovered on Orofino Creek; Mormons establish Idaho's first permanent settlement in Franklin.
1862	Gold is discovered in the Boise Basin.
1863	Idaho Territory is established.
1877	The Nez Perce surrender to U.S. troops near the Canadian border.
1890	Idaho becomes the forty-third U.S. state on July 3.
1914	Moses Alexander is elected governor, becoming the nation's first Jewish governor.
1942	During World War II, Japanese Americans are held at Camp Minidoka.
1951	Near Idaho Falls, electricity is generated from atomic energy for the first time.
1959	Brownlee Dam is completed on the Snake River.
1972	More than ninety miners are killed in an underground fire in the Sunshine Silver Mine.
1976	Eleven people are killed when Teton Dam, near Rexburg, bursts.
1990	Idaho celebrates the 100th anniversary of its statehood.
1996-1997	Idaho suffers from severe floods.

Glossary

environmentalists—people who work to protect wildlife and natural areas

expedition—a journey taken to find, learn, or acquire something

fossil—a form left in stone by an ancient plant or animal

gorge—a deep valley with steep sides

Hispanic—people of Mexican, South American, and other Spanish-speaking cultures

industries—businesses or trades

lava—liquid rock that flows out of a volcano and hardens as it cools

mesas—flat-topped mountains

missionaries—people who travel to new lands to teach religion

pioneers—people who explore or settle in a new land

plateau—high, flat land

reservations—large areas of land set aside for Native Americans

Did You Know?

★ Idaho's name is a made-up word. People used to think it was a Native American name meaning "gem of the mountains." Actually, *Idaho* was the name of a steamship that traveled the Columbia River. After gold was discovered on the Clearwater River in 1860, the site was called the Idaho mines.

★ The entire town of American Falls was moved in the 1920s to make way for the construction of American Falls Dam.

★ Idaho was the last of the fifty states to be explored by Europeans.

★ The village of Island Park has the longest main street in America. It's 33 miles (53 km) long.

★ Appaloosa horses were first bred among the Nez Perce in the Kamiah Valley. They were developed as war horses.

★ More than 6 million gallons (23 million liters) of water gush from Lava Hot Springs every day.

★ Borah Peak, Idaho's highest mountain, grew about 8 inches (20 centimeters) in one day—October 28, 1983. An earthquake caused this sudden growth.

State capital: Boise

State motto: *Esto Perpetua* (Latin for "Let It Be Perpetual")

State nickname: Gem State

Statehood: July 3, 1890; forty-third state

Land area: 82,751 square miles (214,325 sq km); **rank:** eleventh

Highest point: Borah Peak, 12,662 feet (3,862 m) above sea level

Lowest point: The Snake River at Lewiston, 710 feet (216 m) above sea level

Highest recorded temperature: 118°F (48°C) at Orofino on July 28, 1934

Lowest recorded temperature: −60°F (−51°C) at Island Park Dam on January 18, 1943

Average January temperature: 23°F (−5°C)

Average July temperature: 67°F (19°C)

Population in 2000: 1,293,953; **rank:** thirty-ninth

Largest cities in 2000: Boise (185,787), Nampa (51,867), Pocatello (51,466), Idaho Falls (50,730)

Factory products: Electronics equipment, food products, wood products

Farm products: Beef cattle, potatoes, milk, wheat

Mining products: Phosphate rock, silver, sand and gravel

State flag: Idaho's state flag shows the state seal against a blue background. Beneath the seal is a gold-trimmed red banner saying "State of Idaho."

State seal: The state seal shows a female figure holding scales and a spear. They stand for justice and freedom. A male figure with a pick and shovel represents Idaho's mining industry. Between them is an elk's head and a forest scene. They stand for the state's wildlife and forests. Stalks of grain and baskets of fruit represent Idaho's farm products. At the top is a banner with the state motto, *Esto Perpetua.*

State abbreviations: Ida. (traditional); ID (postal)

State Symbols

State bird: Mountain bluebird

State flower: Syringa

State tree: Western white pine

State fish: Cutthroat trout

State horse: Appaloosa

State insect: Monarch butterfly

State fruit: Huckleberry

State vegetable: Potato

State gemstone: Idaho star garnet

State fossil: Hagerman horse fossil

State folk dance: Square dance

Making Idaho Potato Pancakes

Potatoes are a top Idaho crop—and the state vegetable.

Makes six pancakes.

INGREDIENTS:

1 pound Idaho russet potatoes

1 cup chopped onions

2 tablespoons flour

$\frac{1}{2}$ teaspoon salt

$\frac{1}{8}$ teaspoon black pepper

2 eggs, beaten

A little vegetable oil

DIRECTIONS:

Make sure an adult helps you with the chopping and the hot stove. Shred the potatoes using a shredder or grater. Then wrap them in paper towels and squeeze to get any extra liquid out. Mix potatoes, chopped onions, and flour. Add salt, pepper, and beaten eggs, and mix well. Put a little oil in a skillet over medium heat. For each pancake, put $\frac{1}{2}$ cup of the potato mixture in the skillet, and spread it out to about 4 to 6 inches. Cook on one side till brown (about 5 minutes). Turn it over and brown the other side.

"Here We Have Idaho"

Words by Albert J. Tompkins and McKinley Helm, music by Sallie Hume-Douglas

You've heard of the wonders our land does possess,
Its beautiful valleys and hills.
The majestic forests where nature abounds,
We love every nook and rill.

Chorus:
And here we have Idaho,
Winning her way to fame.
Silver and gold in the sunlight blaze,
And romance lies in her name.
Singing, we're singing of you,
Ah, proudly too. All our lives thru,
We'll go singing, singing of you,
Singing of Idaho.
There's truly one state in this great land of ours,
Where ideals can be realized.
The pioneers made it so for you and me,
A legacy we'll always prize.

Famous Idahoans

Joe Albertson (1906–1993) founded a chain of grocery stores in Idaho. Albertsons became one of the largest food and drug store chains in the country.

Gutzon Borglum (1867–1941) was a sculptor. He sculpted four U.S. presidents' heads on Mount Rushmore in the Black Hills of South Dakota. Borglum was born near Bear Lake.

Carol Ryrie Brink (1895–1981) was a children's book author. Her book *Caddie Woodlawn* won the 1936 Newbery Medal. Brink was born in Moscow.

Philo Farnsworth (1906–1971) was an inventor. He invented the television when he was only fourteen years old. He was born in Utah and moved to Idaho as a child.

Vardis Fisher (1895–1968) was an author. Many of his novels tell about frontier days in Idaho. Fisher was born in Annis.

Ernest Hemingway (1899–1961) was an author. His many stories include *For Whom the Bell Tolls* (1940), *The Old Man and the Sea* (1952), and *Islands in the Stream* (1970). In 1954, he received the Nobel Prize for literature. Hemingway (pictured above left) was born in Illinois and later moved to Ketchum, where he died.

Chief Joseph (1840–1904) was a chief of the Nez Perce. Refusing to go to a reservation, he led his people on a long, heroic retreat from the U.S. Army before finally surrendering.

Harmon Killebrew (1936–) is a former star home-run slugger for the Washington Senators, Minnesota Twins, and Kansas City Royals baseball teams. He was elected to the Baseball Hall of Fame in 1984. Killebrew was born in Payette.

Ezra Pound (1885–1972) was a poet who inspired many other poets of the twentieth century. Among his major works is *Cantos,* a long group of poems written over many years (1925–1960). Pound was born in Hailey.

Picabo Street (1971–) is a downhill skier. She won a silver medal for downhill skiing in the 1994 Winter Olympic Games. She went on to win a gold medal in the giant slalom in the 1998 Winter Olympics. Street was born in Triumph.

Lana Turner (1920–1995) was an actress. She played many glamorous movie roles in the 1940s and 1950s. She was born Julia Jean Mildred Frances Turner in Wallace.

Want to Know More?

At the Library

Beatty, Patricia. *Bonanza Girl.* New York: Beech Tree Books, 1993.

Creech, Sharon. *Walk Two Moons.* New York: HarperCollins, 1994.

Hodgkins, Fran. *Idaho.* Mankato, Minn.: Capstone Press, 2003.

Miller, Amy. *Idaho.* Danbury, Conn.: Children's Press, 2003.

Pelta, Kathy. *Idaho.* Minneapolis: Lerner, 1995.

Thompson, Kathleen. *Idaho.* Austin, Tex.: Raintree/Steck-Vaughn, 1996.

On the Web

Access Idaho

http://www.accessidaho.org
To visit the state web site and learn about Idaho's history, government, economy, and laws

Idaho Travel and Tourism

http://www.visitid.org
To find out about Idaho's events, activities, and sights

Idaho State Historical Society

http://www.idahohistory.net
To learn about Idaho's history and historic sites

Through the Mail

Idaho Division of Tourism Development

Department of Commerce
700 West State Street
P.O. Box 83720
Boise, ID 83720
For information on travel and interesting sights in Idaho

Idaho State Historical Society

1109 Main Street, Suite 250
Boise, ID 83720
For information on Idaho's history

On the Road

Idaho State Capitol

Jefferson and Eighth Streets
Boise, ID 83720
208/334-5174
To visit Idaho's state capitol

Index

About the Author

Ann Heinrichs grew up in Fort Smith, Arkansas, and lives in Chicago. She is the author of more than one hundred books for children and young adults on Asian, African, and U.S. history and culture. Ann has also written numerous newspaper, magazine, and encyclopedia articles. She is an award-winning martial artist, specializing in t'ai chi empty-hand and sword forms.

Ann has traveled widely throughout the United States, Africa, Asia, and the Middle East. In exploring each state for this series, she rediscovered the people, history, and resources that make this a great land, as well as the concerns we share with people around the world.